EMMANUEL JOSEPH

From Silence to Roar, The Lost Art of Unamplified Eloquence in a Noisy World

First edition

This book was professionally typeset on Reedsy.
Find out more at reedsy.com

Contents

1

Chapter 1: The Whisper of Beginnings

In a world saturated with noise, silence has become a rare commodity. The art of unamplified eloquence—speaking with clarity, purpose, and authenticity without the crutch of technology—has faded into obscurity. This chapter explores the origins of human communication, when words were crafted carefully and delivered with intention. Before microphones and social media, people relied on the power of their voices and the weight of their words to inspire, persuade, and connect. The whisper of beginnings reminds us that true eloquence is not about volume but about resonance.

The ancients understood the value of silence. Philosophers like Socrates and Confucius emphasized the importance of listening before speaking, of understanding before being understood. Their teachings were not shouted but shared in quiet spaces, where the absence of noise allowed ideas to flourish. This chapter invites readers to reflect on how silence can be a foundation for meaningful communication, a canvas upon which words can be painted with precision and care.

Today, we live in a world where everyone has a platform, yet few have something profound to say. The constant buzz of notifications, the endless stream of opinions, and the pressure to be heard have drowned out the essence of true eloquence. This chapter challenges readers to reclaim the quiet moments, to find their voice not in the cacophony but in the stillness.

The journey from silence to roar begins with a single step: the decision to listen. To listen to oneself, to others, and to the world around us. It is in this act of listening that we discover the power of unamplified eloquence, the ability to speak in a way that moves hearts and minds without the need for amplification.

As we embark on this journey, let us remember that the roar is not born from noise but from the depth of our silence. It is in the quiet that we find our voice, and it is through that voice that we can truly roar.

2

Chapter 2: The Anatomy of a Roar

What makes a roar powerful? Is it the volume, the intensity, or the message it carries? This chapter delves into the anatomy of a roar, breaking down the elements that make unamplified eloquence so compelling. A roar is not merely a loud sound; it is a symphony of passion, clarity, and authenticity. It is the culmination of thought, emotion, and purpose, delivered with conviction.

The first element of a roar is intention. Every word must be chosen with care, every sentence crafted with purpose. Unamplified eloquence demands that we think before we speak, that we consider the impact of our words on others. This chapter explores how intention transforms ordinary speech into extraordinary communication, how it turns whispers into roars.

The second element is presence. In a world distracted by screens and devices, true presence is a rarity. To roar is to be fully present, to connect with your audience on a human level. This chapter emphasizes the importance of eye contact, body language, and emotional engagement in delivering unamplified eloquence.

The third element is authenticity. A roar cannot be faked; it must come from a place of truth. This chapter encourages readers to embrace their unique voice, to speak from the heart rather than conforming to societal expectations. Authenticity is what makes a roar resonate, what makes it unforgettable.

Finally, a roar requires courage. It takes bravery to speak up in a world that often values conformity over individuality. This chapter inspires readers to find their courage, to use their voice to challenge, inspire, and uplift. The anatomy of a roar is not just about speaking; it is about standing tall in the face of silence and making your voice heard.

3

Chapter 3: The Noise That Drowns Us

In this chapter, we confront the enemy of unamplified eloquence: noise. Noise is not just the sound of traffic or the hum of technology; it is the constant barrage of information, opinions, and distractions that fill our lives. Noise drowns out our ability to think, to listen, and to speak with clarity. It is the antithesis of silence, the barrier between us and our true voice.

The digital age has amplified noise to unprecedented levels. Social media, 24-hour news cycles, and the pressure to be constantly connected have created a culture of superficial communication. This chapter examines how noise has eroded our capacity for deep, meaningful conversations and how it has made unamplified eloquence a lost art.

But noise is not just external; it is also internal. The chatter of self-doubt, the fear of judgment, and the need for validation create a cacophony within us that silences our true voice. This chapter encourages readers to identify and quiet their internal noise, to create space for their voice to emerge.

The battle against noise is not easy, but it is necessary. This chapter provides practical strategies for reducing noise in our lives, from digital detoxes to mindfulness practices. By reclaiming our silence, we can rediscover the power of unamplified eloquence.

Noise may be pervasive, but it is not invincible. This chapter reminds readers that they have the power to rise above the noise, to find their voice amidst the chaos. The journey from silence to roar begins with the decision to turn down the volume and listen to the sound of your own voice.

4

Chapter 4: The Power of Pause

In a world that values speed and efficiency, the pause has become a forgotten tool. Yet, it is in the pause that true eloquence is born. This chapter explores the power of the pause, the moment of silence between words that gives them weight and meaning. The pause is not an absence of sound; it is a presence of intention.

The pause allows us to think before we speak, to choose our words with care. It is a sign of confidence, a demonstration that we are in control of our communication. This chapter emphasizes the importance of incorporating pauses into our speech, whether in public speaking, conversations, or even writing.

The pause also creates space for connection. It allows our audience to absorb our words, to reflect on their meaning. In a world that moves at breakneck speed, the pause is a gift—a moment of stillness that fosters understanding and empathy.

This chapter also explores the role of the pause in listening. By pausing before responding, we show respect for the speaker and create an opportunity for deeper dialogue. The pause is a bridge between silence and speech, a tool that enhances both.

The power of the pause is not just in its ability to improve communication; it is in its ability to transform us. By embracing the pause, we become more thoughtful, more intentional, and more eloquent. The pause is the heartbeat of unamplified eloquence, the rhythm that gives our words life.

5

Chapter 5: The Language of the Heart

Eloquence is not just about the mind; it is about the heart. This chapter explores the language of the heart, the emotional depth that gives words their power. Unamplified eloquence is not just about speaking well; it is about speaking with feeling, with empathy, and with love.

The language of the heart is universal. It transcends cultural and linguistic barriers, connecting us on a human level. This chapter examines how emotions like passion, compassion, and vulnerability can elevate our communication, making our words more impactful and memorable.

But speaking from the heart requires courage. It means being open, being real, and being willing to show our true selves. This chapter encourages readers to embrace their emotions, to let their heart guide their words. It is through this authenticity that we can truly connect with others.

The language of the heart also involves listening with empathy. To speak eloquently, we must first understand the emotions of our audience. This chapter provides strategies for tuning into the emotional undercurrents of conversations, for responding with sensitivity and care.

Ultimately, the language of the heart is what makes a roar unforgettable. It is the difference between speaking and being heard, between noise and music. This chapter reminds readers that true eloquence is not just about what we say but how we make others feel.

6

Chapter 6: The Art of Storytelling

Storytelling is the oldest form of human communication, a bridge between silence and speech that has the power to captivate, inspire, and transform. This chapter delves into the art of storytelling as a cornerstone of unamplified eloquence. Stories are not just a means of sharing information; they are a way of connecting with others on a deeply human level.

A great story begins with a moment of silence—a pause that draws the listener in. It is in this silence that curiosity is born, that anticipation builds. This chapter explores how to craft stories that resonate, using vivid imagery, relatable characters, and emotional depth. The power of a story lies not in its complexity but in its authenticity.

Storytelling also requires vulnerability. To tell a story is to share a piece of yourself, to open up to the possibility of judgment or rejection. This chapter encourages readers to embrace vulnerability as a strength, to see it as a pathway to connection. The most powerful stories are those that come from the heart, that reflect our struggles, triumphs, and truths.

But storytelling is not just about speaking; it is also about listening. This chapter emphasizes the importance of being an attentive audience, of creating space for others to share their stories. In a noisy world, the act of listening to a story is a form of unamplified eloquence, a way of honoring the speaker and their message.

The art of storytelling is a reminder that words have the power to change lives. Whether spoken around a campfire, in a boardroom, or on a stage, stories are the threads that weave us together. This chapter inspires readers to become storytellers, to use their voice to create meaning and connection in a fragmented world.

7

Chapter 7: The Discipline of Practice

Unamplified eloquence is not a gift; it is a skill. Like any skill, it requires discipline, dedication, and practice. This chapter explores the role of practice in mastering the art of speaking with clarity and conviction. Practice is not just about repetition; it is about refinement, about honing your voice until it becomes a tool of precision and power.

The first step in practicing unamplified eloquence is self-awareness. This chapter encourages readers to record themselves speaking, to listen to their tone, pace, and choice of words. Self-awareness allows us to identify areas for improvement, to recognize the habits that undermine our communication.

Practice also involves stepping out of your comfort zone. This chapter provides practical exercises for building confidence, from speaking in front of a mirror to joining a public speaking group. The goal is not perfection but progress, to become more comfortable with the sound of your own voice.

But practice is not just about speaking; it is also about listening. This chapter emphasizes the importance of practicing active listening, of tuning into the nuances of conversation. By becoming better listeners, we become better speakers, more attuned to the needs and emotions of our audience.

The discipline of practice is a reminder that unamplified eloquence is a journey, not a destination. It requires patience, persistence, and a willingness to fail. This chapter inspires readers to embrace the process, to see every word as an opportunity to grow and improve.

8

Chapter 8: The Echo of Culture

Culture shapes the way we speak, the way we listen, and the way we connect. This chapter explores the role of culture in unamplified eloquence, examining how cultural norms and values influence our communication. From the directness of Western cultures to the indirectness of Eastern cultures, the way we express ourselves is deeply rooted in our upbringing and environment.

Understanding cultural differences is essential for effective communication. This chapter provides strategies for navigating cultural nuances, from adapting your tone to respecting nonverbal cues. Unamplified eloquence is not about imposing your style of communication but about finding common ground.

Culture also influences the stories we tell and the way we tell them. This chapter examines how cultural narratives shape our identity and our voice, encouraging readers to explore their own cultural heritage as a source of inspiration. By embracing our cultural roots, we can speak with greater authenticity and depth.

But culture is not static; it is constantly evolving. This chapter explores the impact of globalization on communication, from the rise of multiculturalism to the challenges of cultural appropriation. In a world that is increasingly interconnected, unamplified eloquence requires a sensitivity to diversity and inclusion.

The echo of culture is a reminder that our voice is not just our own; it is a reflection of the world we inhabit. This chapter inspires readers to celebrate their cultural identity while remaining open to the perspectives of others, to use their voice as a bridge between worlds.

9

Chapter 9: The Silence Within

The journey from silence to roar is not just about external communication; it is also about internal dialogue. This chapter explores the silence within, the inner world of thoughts, emotions, and beliefs that shape our voice. To speak with eloquence, we must first understand ourselves.

The silence within is a space of reflection, a place where we can confront our fears, doubts, and insecurities. This chapter encourages readers to embrace self-reflection as a tool for growth, to use journaling, meditation, or other practices to connect with their inner voice.

But the silence within is not always peaceful; it can also be chaotic. This chapter examines the role of self-doubt in silencing our voice, providing strategies for overcoming negative self-talk and building self-confidence. Unamplified eloquence begins with self-acceptance, with the belief that our voice matters.

The silence within is also a source of creativity. This chapter explores how moments of stillness can spark inspiration, how the act of listening to ourselves can lead to new ideas and insights. By cultivating inner silence, we create the conditions for our voice to emerge.

Ultimately, the silence within is the foundation of unamplified eloquence. It is the place where we find our truth, our purpose, and our power. This chapter reminds readers that the journey from silence to roar begins within, with the decision to listen to the sound of your own soul.

10

Chapter 10: The Roar of Connection

Unamplified eloquence is not just about speaking; it is about connecting. This chapter explores the roar of connection, the moment when words create a bond between speaker and listener. Connection is the ultimate goal of communication, the reason we speak and listen.

The roar of connection begins with empathy. This chapter emphasizes the importance of understanding the needs, emotions, and perspectives of your audience. Empathy allows us to tailor our message, to speak in a way that resonates with others.

Connection also requires authenticity. This chapter encourages readers to let go of pretense, to speak from the heart rather than from a script. Authenticity builds trust, creating a foundation for meaningful communication.

But connection is not just about words; it is also about presence. This chapter explores the role of body language, eye contact, and tone in creating a sense of connection. Unamplified eloquence is about being fully present, about showing up with your whole self.

The roar of connection is a reminder that communication is a two-way street. This chapter inspires readers to not only speak with eloquence but also to listen with intention, to create a space where others feel heard and valued.

11

Chapter 11: The Future of Unamplified Eloquence

As we stand on the precipice of a digital revolution, the future of unamplified eloquence hangs in the balance. This chapter examines the challenges and opportunities that lie ahead in a world increasingly dominated by technology. Will the human voice be drowned out by algorithms and artificial intelligence, or will it rise above the noise to reclaim its power?

The digital age has brought with it unprecedented tools for communication—social media, podcasts, video conferencing—but it has also created a culture of superficiality. This chapter explores how the immediacy and brevity of digital communication have eroded our capacity for deep, meaningful dialogue. Emojis replace emotions, and hashtags replace heartfelt conversations. Yet, amidst this noise, there is a growing hunger for authenticity, for voices that speak with clarity and purpose.

This chapter also considers the role of technology in amplifying unamplified eloquence. While tools like microphones and recording devices can enhance our reach, they cannot replace the human element of communication. The future of unamplified eloquence lies in striking a balance between leveraging technology and preserving the authenticity of the human voice.

The rise of virtual communication presents both challenges and opportunities. This chapter provides strategies for maintaining connection and presence in a digital world, from mastering the art of video calls to using social media as a platform for meaningful dialogue. The key is to remain grounded in the principles of unamplified eloquence—intention, authenticity, and empathy—even as the medium evolves.

The future of unamplified eloquence is not predetermined; it is shaped by the choices we make today. This chapter inspires readers to be pioneers of a new era of communication, one where the human voice is not lost but elevated, where silence and speech coexist in harmony.

12

Chapter 12: A Call to Roar

The journey from silence to roar is not just a personal one; it is a collective one. This final chapter serves as a call to action, urging readers to reclaim their voice and use it to create a better world. The roar is not just a sound; it is a movement, a declaration that our words matter and that we have the power to make a difference.

This chapter begins with a reflection on the power of collective voices. History is filled with examples of individuals who, through their unamplified eloquence, sparked revolutions, inspired change, and united communities. From Martin Luther King Jr.'s "I Have a Dream" speech to Malala Yousafzai's impassioned advocacy, the roar of one voice can ignite the roar of many.

But a roar is not just about speaking; it is about listening. This chapter emphasizes the importance of creating spaces where diverse voices can be heard, where dialogue can flourish. The true power of unamplified eloquence lies in its ability to foster understanding and connection, to bridge divides and build bridges.

This chapter also provides practical steps for readers to begin their own journey from silence to roar. From practicing active listening to finding opportunities to speak up, the path to unamplified eloquence is one of intention and action. It is a journey that requires courage, vulnerability, and a commitment to growth.

Finally, this chapter reminds readers that the roar is not an end but a beginning. It is a reminder that our voice is a gift, one that can inspire, heal, and transform. The world is waiting for your roar—not just the sound of your voice, but the power of your truth.

21

13

Epilogue: The Echo of Your Roar

As the book concludes, the epilogue reflects on the lasting impact of unamplified eloquence. The echo of your roar is not confined to the moment you speak; it reverberates through time, touching lives and shaping futures. Your voice, no matter how quiet or loud, has the power to create ripples of change.

The journey from silence to roar is not easy, but it is worth it. It is a journey of self-discovery, of connection, and of purpose. It is a reminder that in a noisy world, the most powerful sound is the one that comes from within.

So, take a deep breath. Listen to the silence. And when you are ready, let your roar be heard.

From Silence to Roar: The Lost Art of Unamplified Eloquence in a Noisy World is not just a book; it is an invitation—to speak, to listen, and to connect. It is a reminder that in a world filled with noise, the most powerful sound is the one that comes from the heart.

Book Description: From Silence to Roar: The Lost Art of Unamplified Eloquence in a Noisy World

In a world that never stops talking, true communication has become a rarity. We live in an age of constant noise—social media feeds buzzing, notifications pinging, and voices clamoring for attention. Yet, amidst this cacophony, the art of unamplified eloquence—the ability to speak with clarity, purpose, and authenticity without the crutch of technology—has been all but forgotten.

From Silence to Roar is a journey back to the essence of human connection. It is a call to reclaim the power of your voice, not through volume or amplification, but through intention, presence, and authenticity. This book explores the profound beauty of silence, the discipline of listening, and the courage it takes to speak from the heart.

Through 12 thought-provoking chapters, you'll discover:

- How silence can be the foundation of meaningful communication.
- The anatomy of a roar—what makes words truly powerful.
- Practical strategies to cut through the noise and find your authentic voice.
- The role of storytelling, empathy, and cultural understanding in creating connection.
- How to navigate the challenges of a digital world while staying true to the art of unamplified eloquence.

This is not just a book about speaking; it's about being heard. It's about understanding that the most powerful communication doesn't come from shouting louder but from speaking with depth and resonance. It's about realizing that your voice, no matter how quiet, has the power to inspire, to heal, and to transform.

From Silence to Roar is for anyone who has ever felt drowned out by the noise, who has struggled to find their voice, or who longs to connect more deeply with others. It's a guide, a manifesto, and an invitation to rediscover the lost art of unamplified eloquence—and to let your roar echo in the hearts of those who hear it.

Are you ready to turn down the noise, listen to the silence, and unleash the power of your voice? The world is waiting for your roar.